KURT WEILL SONGS

A Centennial Anthology

VOLUME 1

D1591443

Project Manager: Sy Feldman
Compiled by Edward Harsh and Dave Stein
Production Coordinator: Donna Salzburg
Book Art Layout: Jorge Paredes

The Kurt Weill Foundation for Music, which conceived this collection for the centenary celebration of Kurt Weill's birth, is grateful for the cooperation of its publishing partners, Warner/Chappell Music, European American Music Corp., Universal Edition, and The Richmond Organization, in making this project possible. Photos and sheet music originals were provided courtesy of the Weill-Lenya Research Center (www.kwf.org).

PREFACE

KURT WEILL SONGS
A Centennial Anthology

From a point early in his career, Kurt Weill showed an affinity for the dramatic use of songs as integral parts of his musical theater pieces. Many such songs were published individually at the time of each piece's premiere, but only a handful have remained available in recent years. This anthology makes the collection accessible in its entirety for the first time. Included here, in two volumes, is each and every song from a Weill theater piece that was published individually during the composer's lifetime. The music is reprinted from the historical sheet music itself, so the user can see in the format and presentation graphic analogies to the many steps in the composer's life journey: Berlin, Paris, London, New York, Hollywood, and so on.

The timing of this publication is significant in a number of ways. For one, it appears on the eve of a new century and millennium. That alone is enough to inspire a look back on the noteworthy music produced in the previous hundred years. But the year 2000 has special meaning in relation to Kurt Weill. It marks the hundredth anniversary of his birth and the fiftieth anniversary of his death.

This centennial comes at an especially propitious moment for rediscovery of the composer's work. The steady growth since the 1950s of interest in his life and music has accelerated in recent years. As people discover the remarkable range of Weill's accomplishment, both in the variety and quality of his work, the demand to hear and experience the music increases with each passing year. The celebration in 2000 will see the greatest number yet of Weill performances, of pieces both famous and unfamiliar. This exposure to the composer's full oeuvre—very much like the opportunity provided by this anthology—will encourage a fuller understanding of the composer and his creations and perhaps a greater appreciation of the character and depth of his contribution to music in the extraordinary century now past.

KURT WEILL BIOGRAPHY

Early in his life, Kurt Weill found his calling in the musical theater. As a youth he staged homemade shows in a hall connected to the synagogue where his father served as cantor. By the time he was twenty he had gained extensive experience as a rehearsal accompanist and assistant conductor in local theaters and opera houses. And he already knew that the compositions that were beginning to spill forth from his pen were inspired by more than music alone. In a letter to his brother he wrote, "I need poetry to set my imagination into motion; my imagination isn't a bird, it's an airplane." In slightly less than three decades as a professional composer, he wrote more than thirty works for the stage. By the time the first few had been completed, he had already established three practices that would remain characteristic of his work throughout his career: exploration of new models and forms, use of elements drawn from popular music, and collaboration with the finest contemporary playwrights. He remained persistent in his determined lifelong quest to advance the cause of musical theater despite the uncertainties and dislocations he experienced in his short but eventful life.

Born in Dessau, Germany, March 2, 1900, Weill enjoyed great prominence as a young composer in his native land. He was seen as one of the bright lights of his generation, along with such peers as Paul Hindemith and Ernst Krenek. Success came quickly: acclaim for his one-act opera *Der Protagonist (The Protagonist)* in Dresden in 1926; a noteworthy scandal in Baden-Baden in 1927 attending the *Mahagonny Songspiel*, his first collaboration with Bertolt Brecht; topping it

all, the sensational triumph of *Die Dreigroschenoper (The Threepenny Opera)* from its very first performance in 1928. He skillfully played each accomplishment into more opportunity and used those opportunities to continue his lifelong quest, creating new musical theater works both beautiful and serious. Indeed, this very seriousness began to cause him trouble.

His works of the early 1930s, such as *Aufstieg und Fall der Stadt Mahagonny (Rise and Fall of the City of Mahagonny)*, *Die Bürgschaft (The Pledge)*, and *Der Silbersee (The Silver Lake)* (with texts by Brecht, Caspar Neher, and Georg Kaiser respectively), confronted directly some of the most divisive political issues of the day. Performances of these works, although well received by critics and public, were greeted with anger and derision (sometimes violently demonstrated) by the Nazis and their growing ranks of supporters. By the time Adolf Hitler became chancellor of Germany in January 1933, Weill was distinctly *persona non grata* and he knew it. He fled to Paris, never again to set foot in the country of his birth, the scene of his remarkable early success.

The years in France were not easy ones. He was suddenly an *emigré*, an outsider trying to fit in. He and his wife of seven years, actress-singer Lotte Lenya, divorced. Still, he continued to compose with his usual productivity. He briefly renewed his collaboration with Brecht to produce *Die sieben Todsünden (The Seven Deadly Sins)*, a "ballet with singing" for George Balanchine's troupe "Les Ballets 1933." There were also cabaret chansons, a score for Jacques Deval's *Marie Galante*, and an adaptation for British audiences of his operetta *Der Kuhhandel* (libretto by Robert Vambery), newly titled *A Kingdom for a Cow*.

In September 1935, Weill (now reunited with Lenya) set out for New York on what was intended to be a professional visit of only a few months. It turned out to be the first move towards a wholehearted embrace of the United States that would end with naturalization as an American citizen in 1943. The original reason for the trip was to oversee famed director Max Reinhardt's production of Franz Werfel's biblical epic *Der Weg der Verheissung (The Road of Promise),* for which Weill had written an extensive oratorio-like score. A shortened version of the work finally reached the stage as *The Eternal Road* in January 1937. In the meantime Weill had collaborated with Paul Green and the progressive Group Theatre on a new anti-war play, *Johnny Johnson*. Encouraged by what he saw as the possibilities offered by commercial theater in America, he and Lenya (remarried in January 1937) decided to stay.

Weill continued to demonstrate an uncanny ability to find interesting projects, through which he began to develop a reputation as a skilled craftsman in the world of the American musical theater. He collaborated with the prominent playwright Maxwell Anderson on *Knickerbocker Holiday*. He worked in Hollywood, composing the score for Fritz Lang's film *You and Me*. A commission from the organizers of the 1939 New York World's Fair resulted in *Railroads on Parade,* a pageant on a grand scale that proved to be one of the big successes of the event.

In the early 1940s, the two Broadway hits *Lady in the Dark* (book by Moss Hart and lyrics by Ira Gershwin) and *One Touch of Venus* (book by S. J. Perelman and lyrics by Ogden Nash) firmly established Weill as a new and original voice in the American musical theater. Further, they gave him the credibility to take new risks in continuing his lifelong quest. Following a brief foray into film musicals with *Where Do We Go From Here?* (lyrics by Ira Gershwin), his next project, the satirical operetta *The Firebrand of Florence,* was troubled by a host of problems, from book to casting, and closed after a disappointing forty-three performances. His next major projects, however, set a high standard as bold (and successful) ventures.

First came *Street Scene* (book by Elmer Rice and lyrics by Langston Hughes), his ambitious "American Opera" in the tradition of *Porgy and Bess*; then *Love Life* (book and lyrics by Alan Jay Lerner), now recognized as the first "concept musical"; then *Lost in the Stars* (book and lyrics by Maxwell Anderson), based on Alan Paton's anti-apartheid novel *Cry the Beloved Country.* In between, his one-act folk opera *Down in the Valley* had begun its run of several hundred productions in schools and communities around the nation. Early in 1950 Weill began to sketch songs for a new collaboration with Anderson based upon Mark Twain's *The Adventures of Huckleberry Finn.* His work was cut short by a heart attack, and he died a few weeks later on April 3, one month past his fiftieth birthday.

KURT WEILL

Contents

Contents

KURT WEILL

KURT WEILL

Tableau from the Weill-Brecht opera *Aufstieg und Fall der Stadt Mahagonny*. The disreputable denizens of Mahagonny are seeking liberation from all rules, symbolized by the sign "Es ist verbot" (That is forbidden).

A crowd scene from the first act finale of *The Firebrand of Florence*, New York, 1945.

Macheath (Harald Paulsen) on the gallows just before he is reprieved. Tiger Brown (Kurt Gerron) holds the rope as Polly Peachum (Roma Bahn) and Mr. Peachum (Erich Ponto) look on. From the original production of *The Threepenny Opera* at the Theater am Schiffbauerdamm, Berlin, 1928.

Lilian Holliday, the plucky heroine of *Happy End*, holds a Salvation Army banner, from the original production in Berlin, 1929.

MAHAGONNY

ALABAMA SONG

Lyrics by
BERTOLT BRECHT

Music by
KURT WEILL

12

ALL AT ONCE

Lyrics by
IRA GERSHWIN

Music by
KURT WEILL

All at Once - 4 - 1

APPLE JACK

Lyrics by
MAXWELL ANDERSON

Music by
KURT WEILL

Apple Jack - 3 - 1

18

said "La - dy, ma'am, I beg par - don, Would you
goes down so fine when you're thirs - ty, She ___
noth - in' but ap - ple," says Sa - tan, "It's just
an - swered, "I'm not ver - y thirs - ty But I'll

try this here juice from my jug?"
hangs on and tips from the jug up.
noth - in' but plain ap - ple jack."
drink it be - cause you're my dear."

Refrain

It was ap - ple, ap - ple, ap - ple, It was

ap - ple, ap - ple, ap - ple,___ jack, Oh,

once you reach out for that poi - son The___

dev - il's on your track.

2. Now she track.___
3. What is
4. Then this

AS LONG AS I LOVE

Text by
ROBERT VAMBERY
English Lyrics by
DESMOND CARTER

Music by
KURT WEILL

As long as I love___ I live for

my love.___ The man I sigh for___ I'm rea-dy to die for.___

As Long as I Love - 4 - 1

AUF NACH MAHAGONNY

Lyrics by
BERTOLT BRECHT

Music by
KURT WEILL

Jack

schon,   dort gibt____ es fri-schen Fleisch-sa-lat und   kei - ne Di - rek - tion.

Alle

p

Schö - ner   grü - ner   Mond von A - la-ba - ma,   leuch - te

uns,   denn wir ha-ben heu - te hier   un-term Hemde Geld - pa - pier

mf

für   ein   gro - ßes   Lachen deines gro-ßen dum-men Munds.

p

f

un-term Hem-de Geld - pa - pier für ein gro - ßes

La-chen dei-nes gro-ßen dum-men Munds.

DER BÄCKER BACKT UMS MORGENROT

Text by
GEORG KAISER

Music by
KURT WEILL

30

31

Der Bäcker backt ums Morgenrot - 6 - 3

S.

Schnal - le Dei-nen Gür - tel en - ger um ein Loch!

4 Burschen

Es geht noch, es geht noch, es geht ja im-mer noch;

S.

Schnal - le Dei-nen Gür - tel en - ger um ein Loch!

4. B.

Erst denkt man, es geht nicht und dann geht's doch.

Severin

Und so ver-geht die Le - bens-zeit, man war doch da; man

war be- reit, man war da und man war be - reit. Doch will sich wer be schwe ren, muß er

hö - ren, muß er hö - ren, was man ihm in die Oh - ren schreit, was man

ihm in die Oh - ren schreit!

Schnal-le Dei-nen Gür - tel en - ger um ein Loch, es geht noch, es geht noch, es geht ja im-mer noch!

4 Burschen

Schnal-le Dei-nen Gür - tel en - ger um ein Loch, es geht noch, es geht noch, es geht ja im-mer noch!

Schnal-le Dei-nen Gür - tel en - ger um ein Loch, erst denkt man es geht nicht, erst denkt man es geht nicht, erst

Schnal-le Dei-nen Gür - tel en - ger um ein Loch, erst denkt man es geht nicht, erst denkt man es geht nicht, erst

Poco tenuto

denkt man es geht nicht und dann geht's doch.

denkt man es geht nicht und dann geht's doch.

Poco tenuto

BALLAD OF THE ROBBERS

Lyrics by
MAXWELL ANDERSON

Music by
KURT WEILL

Ballad of the Robbers - 4 - 1

so the hon-est men sat down_ A - round a pot of ale, And made a law that all the thieves should be con-fined to jail. Where - at the thieves were all con-fined_ Be - hind those dis - mal bars_ So hon-est men_ could walk a-broad_ For bus-i-ness-es, or wars. But then there was a clev-

er thief— Who up and said said he The hon-est men have grown—

— so few,— So nu-mer-ous are we. But if we band to -geth-

— er now,— A-gainst the hon-est men, The hon-est men will go to jail,—

And we'll go free a - gain.

38

Ballad of the Robbers - 4 - 4

BALLADE VOM ANGENEHMEN LEBEN

Lyrics by
BERTOLT BRECHT

Music by
KURT WEILL

Le - ben le - be, wer da mag! ich ha - be (un -ter uns) ge - nug da -

von, kein Vö - gel-chen von hier bis Ba - by - lon ver -

trü - ge die - se Kost nur ei - nen Tag. Was hilft da Frei - heit, es ist nicht be -

quem, nur wer im Wohlstand lebt, lebt an - ge - nehm. Die

A - ben-teu-rer mit dem küh-nen We-sen   und ih-rer Gier, die Haut zum Markt zu

tra-gen,   die stets so frei sind und die Wahr-heit sa-gen,   da -

mit die Spie-ßer et - was Küh-nes le-sen: wenn man sie sieht, wie das am A-bend

friert,   mit kal-ter Gat-tin stumm zu Bet - te geht   und

42

M. horcht, ob niemand klatscht und nichts ver-steht und trostlos in das Jahr fünf-tau-send

M. stiert. Jetzt frag ich Sie nun noch: ist das be-quem? Nur wer im

M. Wohlstand lebt, lebt an-ge-nehm. Ich sel-ber könn-te mich durch-aus be-

M. grei-fen, wenn ich mich lie-ber groß und ein-sam sä-he, doch

Ballade vom angenehmen Leben - 5 - 5

BALLADE VON CÄSARS TOD

Text by
GEORG KAISER

Music by
KURT WEILL

48

Ballade von Cäsars Tod - 5 - 5

DIE DREIGROSCHENOPER

BALLADE VON DER SEXUELLEN HÖRIGKEIT

Lyrics by
BERTOLT BRECHT

Music by
KURT WEILL

Andante quasi largo

Gesang

Piano

1. Da ist nun ei - ner schon der Sa - tan
2. So man - cher Mann sah man - chen Mann ver -

sel - ber, der Metz - ger: er und al - le an - dern: Käl - ber! Der frech - ste
rek - ken: Ein gro - ßer Geist blieb in 'ner Hu - re stek - ken! Und die's mit -

Hund! Der schlimm - ste Hu - ren - trei - ber! Wer kocht ihn ab, der al - le ab - kocht?
an - sahn, was sie sich auch schwu - ren_ als sie ver - reck - ten, wer be - grub sie?

Ballade von der sexuellen Hörigkeit - 3 - 1

50

Wei - ber. Das fragt nicht, ob er will, er ist be - reit.
Hu - ren. Das fragt nicht, ob sie woll'n, sie sind be - reit.

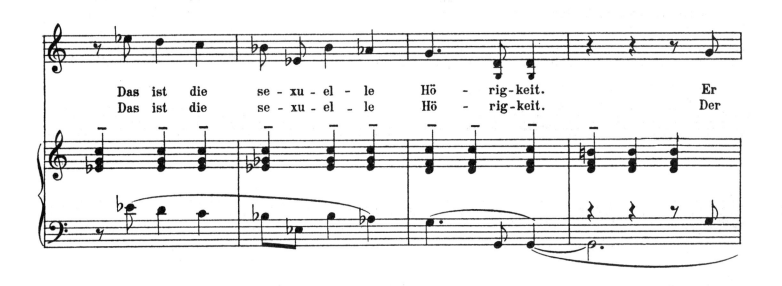

Das ist die se - xu - el - le Hö - rig - keit. Er
Das ist die se - xu - el - le Hö - rig - keit. Der

glaubt nicht an die Bi - bel, nicht ans B. G. B. Er meint, er ist der größ - te
hält sich an die Bi - bel, der ans B. G. B. Ein Mann_ ein Christ! Ein Jud_ ein

51

E - go - ist. Weiß, daß wer'n Weib sieht, schon ver - scho - ben ist und läßt kein
An - ar - chist! Am Mit - tag zwingt man sich daß man nicht Sell' - rie frißt, nach - mit - tags

Weib in sei - ne Näh_ Er soll den
weiht man sich noch 'ner I - dee. Am A - bend

Tag nicht vor dem A - bend lo - ben, denn vor es Nacht wird, liegt er wie - der
sagt man: mit mir geht's nach o - ben. Und vor es Nacht wird, liegt man wie - der

dro - ben.
dro - ben.

Ballade von der sexuellen Hörigkeit - 3 - 3

DIE DREIGROSCHENOPER

BARBARA SONG

Lyrics by
BERTOLT BRECHT

Music by
KURT WEILL

Moderato assai (♩ = 63)

Polly

Einst glaub-te ich, als ich noch un-schul-dig war, und das war ich einst grad so wie du,_ viel-leicht kommt auch zu_ mir ein-mal ei-ner und dann muß ich wis-sen,was ich tu. Und wenn er Geld hat-te, und wenn er nett war und sein Kra-gen war auch werktags rein, und wenn er wuß-te, was sich bei ei-ner Da-me schickt_ dann sag-te ich ihm:

poco rit.

Barbara Song - 6 - 1

53

Barbara Song - 6 - 2

Moderato assai

Der er - ste, der kam, war ein Mann aus Kent, der war wie ein Mann sein soll. Der zwei - te __ hat - te drei Schif - fe im Ha - fen und der drit - te __ war nach mir toll. Und als sie Geld hat - ten und als sie nett wa - ren und ihr Kra - gen war auch werktags rein, und als sie wuß - ten, was sich bei ei - ner Da - me schickt, da sag - te ich ih - nen: Nein. Da be - hielt ich mei - nen

accel.

poco rit.

f Più animato

BERLIN IM LICHT

Music and Lyrics by
KURT WEILL

Slow-Fox

Piano

Und zum Spa - zie - ren-gehn ge - nügt das

Son - nen-licht, doch um die Stadt Ber - lin zu sehn, ge - nügt die Son - ne nicht,

das ist kein lau - schi - ges Plätz-chen, das

Berlin im Licht - 3 - 1

ist 'ne zie-mli-che Stadt._____ Da-mit man da___ al-les gut

se-hen kann,___ da braucht man schon__ ei-ni-ge Watt.___

p
Na' wat denn? Na wat denn? Was is das für 'ne Stadt denn?

REFRAIN
Komm, mach mal Licht, da-mit man sehn kann, ob was da ist, komm, mach mal Licht und

f

60

re - de nun mal nicht. Komm, mach mal Licht, dann wollen wir doch auch mal se - hen,

ob das 'ne Sa-che ist: Berlin im Licht. Komm, mach mal Licht, da-mit man

sehn kann, ob was da ist, komm, mach mal Licht und re - de nun mal

nicht. Komm, mach mal Licht, dann wol - len wir doch auch mal se - hen,

ob das 'ne Sa - che ist: Ber - lin in Licht.

BIG MOLE

Lyrics by
MAXWELL ANDERSON

Music by
KURT WEILL

Big

Mole was a dig-ger of the fast-est — kind, He'd dig in the earth like you
Mole was a youn - ker, they show'd him a mine, He said "I — like the i -

think in your mind; When — Big Mole came to the side of a hill In —
de - a — fine. Let me have that hose, let me have that — drill" If they

Big Mole - 5 - 1

64

Big Mole - 5 - 5

BILBAO SONG

Lyrics by
BERTOLT BRECHT

Music by
KURT WEILL

Bills Ball-haus in Bil - ba - o, Bil - ba-o, Bil - ba - o war das

schön - ste auf dem gan - zen Kon - ti - nent. Dort gab's für ei - nen Dol - lar Krach und

Won - ne, Krach und Won - ne, Krach und Won - ne und was die Welt ihr Ei - gen nennt.

A - ber wenn Sie da her - ein - ge-kom-men wä - ren, ich weiß nicht, ob Ih - nen so was grad ge -

Wo noch die Lie-be lohnt__

(gesprochen)

Lang, lang ist's her!

Ich weiß ja nicht, ob Ih-nen

so was grad ge-fällt, doch__ es war das Schön-ste, es war das Schön - ste,

es war das Schön - ste auf der Welt.

A BOY LIKE YOU

Lyrics by
LANGSTON HUGHES

Music by
KURT WEILL

Lyrics: crowd. Such a man-ly arm I'll have to lean on When I walk down the A-ve-nue. Some-bod-y will al-ways be my stand-by, Who do you think it is? Guess who? Some-bod-y I know will al-ways

A Boy Like You - 4 - 3

72

THE CATFISH SONG

Lyrics by
MAXWELL ANDERSON

Music by
KURT WEILL

The Catfish Song - 3 - 1

74

The Catfish Song - 3 - 2

75

The Catfish Song - 3 - 3

COME IN, MORNIN'

Lyrics by
MAXWELL ANDERSON

Music by
KURT WEILL

Come in mornin', Come in sun.___ Time is a - born - in', Day has be - gun.___ Ex - cuse this house with - out ceil - ing or floors, And it's hav - in' no walls and it's all out - doors. It

Come In, Mornin' - 3 - 1

Come In, Mornin' - 3 - 2

COMPLAINTE DE LA SEINE

Lyrics by
MAURICE MAGRE

Music by
KURT WEILL

Complainte de la Seine - 3 - 1

vie... Et puis des cailloux et des bê_tes gri_ses... L'â_me des é_gouts soufflant des poi_sons... Les an_

_neaux je_tés par des in_com_pri_ses, Des pieds qu'une hé_li_ce a cou_pés du tronc...

Et les fruits maudits des ven_tres sté_ri_les, Les blancs a_vortés que nul n'ai_ma...

Les vomis_sements de la grand' vil_le... Au fond de la Seine, il y a ce_la... O Sei_ne clé_

_men_te où_vont les ca_da_vres, O lit dont les draps sont faits de li_mon, Fleuv' des dé_

DANCE AROUND THE GOLDEN CALF

Text by
FRANZ WERFEL

Music by
KURT WEILL

Dance Around the Golden Calf - 4 - 1

Dance Around the Golden Calf - 4 - 2

84

A God of Gold, who is like us, no God of soul! _____ This is a

God! This is a God! This is a God!

This is a God! This is a home-ly God! This is a

shin-ing God! This is a kind-ly God!

DAVID'S PSALM

Text by
FRANZ WERFEL

Music by
KURT WEILL

David's Psalm - 2 - 1

moun - tains danced joy - ous Like rams in the spring, The _

hills were like lambs when shep - herd boys sing.

O - cean, why_ fleest thou, Jor - dan, why_ seest thou, Moun - tain, what wings thee,

Hill, _ what brings thee. Al - le - lu - jah, Al - le - lu - jah!

DENN WIE MAN SICH BETTET, SO LIEGT MAN

Lyrics by
BERTOLT BRECHT

Music by
KURT WEILL

Jen. mir! Was aus mir noch wird, das wer-den wir seh'n! Ein Mensch ist kein
fragt, da muß man sei-ne kurze Zeit be - nüt - zen! Ein Mensch ist kein

rit. a tempo *(ruhig)*

Jen. Tier! _____ 1. 2. Denn
Tier! _____

Jen. wie man sich bet - tet, so liegt man, es deckt ei - nen

Jen. kei - ner da zu und __ wenn ei - ner tritt, dann bin

DIRGE FOR A SOLDIER

Lyrics by
MAXWELL ANDERSON

Music by
KURT WEILL

Drawn to the earth the sol - dier lies, With beat of drum we ush - er him home.

Emp - tied of mirth his blind - ed eyes

Stare at the grass roots whence we come.

Dirge for a Soldier - 4 - 1

92

Dirge for a Soldier - 4 - 2

94

ONE TOUCH OF VENUS (FILM)

DON'T LOOK NOW

Lyrics by
ANN RONELL

Music by
KURT WEILL

Don't Look Now - 4 - 1

ECONOMICS

Lyrics by
ALAN JAY LERNER

Music by
KURT WEILL

lev - en a day.___ Now that's good e - co - no - mics,

That's good e - co - no - mics, That's good e - co - no - mics, but

aw - ful bad for love. Now Sa - rah and her

hus - band, they were do - in' O - kay, For Sa - rah had an

102

Economics - 6 - 4

104

Economics - 6 - 6

MARIE GALANTE

LES FILLES DE BORDEAUX

Lyrics by
JACQUES DEVAL

Music by
KURT WEILL

Les filles de Bordeaux - 3 - 1

De _ vant Ca _ pis _ tra _ no, Sur la mer O _ cé _ a _ ne.
Chercher d'autres pu _ tains Sur la terre é _ tran _ gè _ re.

REFRAIN

Les __ fil _____ les de Bor _ deaux _____ Qui s'en

vont _____ sur la va _____ gue F'raient __ mieux __

__ de _ s'foutre à l'eau _____ Sans sor _ tir _____ de Bé _

FOOLISH HEART

Lyrics by
OGDEN NASH

Music by
KURT WEILL

love used to touch me so light - ly Why will my heart be - tray me so?___ I would dance with a new lov - er night - ly___ But my fool - ish heart says no. ___ Love no. ___

Foolish Heart - 4 - 4

GIRL OF THE MOMENT

Lyrics by
IRA GERSHWIN

Music by
KURT WEILL

Girl of the Moment - 4 - 1

* *Names of chords for Ukulele and Banjo.*
  Symbols for Guitar.

LE GRAND LUSTUCRU

Lyrics by
JACQUES DEVAL

Music by
KURT WEILL

Le grand Lustucru - 3 - 1

GREEN-UP TIME

Lyrics by
ALAN JAY LERNER

Music by
KURT WEILL

Green-Up Time - 4 - 1

LOVE LIFE

HERE I'LL STAY

Lyrics by
ALAN JAY LERNER

Music by
KURT WEILL

If I've no will to go from home; Or have no urge the seas to roam; Or turn my back on a dis-tant star and nev-er burn to wan-der far; It's not be-cause of fear. It's be-cause my goal is clear. ___

Here I'll Stay - 4 - 1

Here I'll Stay - 4 - 3

smile all day through. _____ But I know well they're

wrong and I know where I be - long, And

here I'll stay with you. _____ For that

land is a sand - y il - lu - sion; _____

HOW CAN YOU TELL AN AMERICAN?

Lyrics by
MAXWELL ANDERSON

Music by
KURT WEILL

128

Refrain

is-n't that he's short or tall ___ It is-n't that he's round or flat ___
is-n't that he's good or bad ___ It is-n't that he's gay or grim ___

___ It is-n't that he's civ-il-ized or ab-o-rig-i-nal Nor the
___ It's on-ly that au-thor-i-ty re-pels him as a lad And

head size of his hat ___ No, it's just that he hates and e-
nev-er goes down with him ___ Yes it's just that he hates Both the

ter-nal-ly de-spis-es The po-lice-man on his beat And the judge at his as-siz-es. *Irv:* The
guts and the fac-es of the peo-ple who can or-der him and put him through his pac-es. *Br:* The as-

130

132

HOW MUCH I LOVE YOU

Lyrics by
OGDEN NASH

Music by
KURT WEILL

How Much I Love You - 3 - 1

ICH BIN EINE ARME VERWANDTE

Text by
GEORG KAISER

Music by
KURT WEILL

Fennimore

Ich bin ei - ne ar - me Ver - wand - te und ge -

hö - re zu An-dern da - zu,

(gesprochen) Ach, wenn sich doch keiner um mich kümmern wollte!

doch

das tu - en On-kel und Tan - te und nichts freut sie, was ich auch tu': _____ Das ist kein

Ich bin eine arme Verwandte - 4 - 1

Le - ben, das ist nur Ver - druß, den man, was soll denn wer - den, er - tra - gen muß.

Ich hab' ei - nen Kof - fer voll Ha - be, den schlep - pe ich ü - ber - all hin,

(gesprochen) Ach, wenn ich mich doch seiner entledigen könnte!

weil ich mir die Fin - ger wund scha - be und auch nicht die kräftigste bin. Und nirgends will man mich be - hal - ten, weil

138

IF LOVE REMAINS

Lyrics by
IRA GERSHWIN

Music by
KURT WEILL

If Love Remains - 5 - 1

mind those cars and planes If love re-mains.

Oh, the fu-ture looks be-wild-'rin' All the

shapes of things to be! But so long as there are homes and

flow-ers and chil-dren. The fu-ture is all right with me. Think of

BILL

144

I'M A STRANGER HERE MYSELF

Lyrics by
OGDEN NASH

Music by
KURT WEILL

I'm a Stranger Here Myself - 8 - 1

146

I'm a Stranger Here Myself - 8 - 2

148

I'm a Stranger Here Myself - 8 - 4

IS IT HIM OR IS IT ME?

Lyrics by
ALAN JAY LERNER

Music by
KURT WEILL

Is It Him or Is It Me? - 6 - 1

I nev-er dreamed

I'd see the

day,

But may-be he is right

We're

bet - ter off this way.

No, I'm not going to cry, I won't, what's done is

Refrain Andante non troppo (*Blues tempo*)

156

Now who's to blame it's dead and o - ver, Is it him or is it me?

We used to share our ev - 'ry mo - ment,

We were as close as two can be.

IT NEVER WAS YOU

Lyrics by
MAXWELL ANDERSON

Music by
KURT WEILL

It Never Was You - 4 - 1

* *Diagrams for Guitar Accomp.*

J'ATTENDS UN NAVIRE

Lyrics by
JACQUES DEVAL

Music by
KURT WEILL

J'attends un navire - 5 - 1

REFRAIN FINAL

a Tempo

...tends un na-vi-re Qui vien-dra Et pour le con-dui-re, Ce na-vire

a Tempo

à Le vent de mon cœur qui sou-pi-re L'eau de mes pleurs le porte-

allarg.

a Tempo

-ra; Et si la mer veut le dé-trui-re, Ce na-vi-

allarg.

a Tempo

-re qui vien-dra, Je le por-té-rai, ce na-vi-re, Jus-qu'à

ff

Bor-deaux en-tre mes bras.

ff

JE NE T'AIME PAS

Lyrics by
MAURICE MAGRE

Music by
KURT WEILL

Je ne t'aime pas - 2 - 1

KANONEN SONG

Lyrics by
BERTOLT BRECHT

Music by
KURT WEILL

KÖNNEN EINEM TOTEN MANN NICHT HELFEN

Lyrics by
BERTOLT BRECHT

Music by
KURT WEILL

Bill

Kön-nen ihm Es-sig ho-len, kön-nen sein Ge-sicht ab-rei-ben, kön-nen die Beiß-zan-ge ho-len, kön-nen ihm die Zun-ge her-aus-ziehn, kön-nen ei-nem to-ten Mann nicht hel-(fen)

Chor (Bill's Zug)

Kön-nen ei-nem to-ten Mann nicht hel-fen, kön-nen einem to-ten Mann nicht

Moses **f**
Kön-nen ihm gut

hel - fen.

zu - reden, können ihn an - brüllen, können ihn lie-gen lassen, kön-nen ihn

Männer (beide Züge)

mit - nehmen, können ei-nem to-ten Mann kei-ne Vorschriften machen. Können ei-nem to-ten Mann nicht

hel - fen,

Kön - nen ei - nem to - ten Mann nicht hel - fen.
Begbick
Kön-nen ihm Geld in die Hand drük-ken, kön-nen ihm ein
Loch gra - ben, kön-nen ihn hin - ein - stop - fen, kön - nen ihm die
Schau - fel hin - auf - hau'n, kön - nen ei - nem to - ten Mann nicht hel-(fen.)

The Threepenny Opera triumphed off Broadway in 1954. Here, a publicity photo from that production, showing Mack the Knife (Scott Merrill), Polly (Jo Sullivan) and Jenny (Lotte Lenya).

KRANICHE-DUETT

Lyrics by
BERTOLT BRECHT

Music by
KURT WEILL

Kraniche-Duett - 6 - 1

180

Kraniche-Duett - 6 - 3

LIEBESLIED

Lyrics by
BERTOLT BRECHT

Music by
KURT WEILL

Liebeslied - 2 - 1

LIED VON DEN BRAUNEN INSELN

Lyrics by
LION FEUCHTWANGER

Music by
KURT WEILL

1. Das ist von den brau - - nen In - seln das Lied, die
2. sind die___ brau - nen___ In - seln, mein Jung, die
3. kommt ist ge - sund und wer geht ist ge - schwächt. Die
4. tro - le - um stinkt und die In - sel___ stinkt. Sie

1. Män - ner sind schlecht und die Wei - ber sind krank. Und ei - ne
2. Wei - ber sind krank und die Män - ner sind schlecht. Ei - ne Äf - fin hält
3. Äf - fin re - giert in___ Bett und Fa - brik. Die Äf - fin hat
4. stinkt___ nach gel - bem und schwar - zem Mann. Doch der Dol - lar stinkt

1. Äf - fin macht dort den Be - trieb und die Fel - der ver - dor - ren im
2. dort das___ Gan - ze in Schwung. Und wer kommt ist ge - sund, und wer
3. Geld und die Äf - fin hat Recht und das Manns - volk pa - riert___ in
4. nicht, den das Erd - öl___ bringt und ge - gen die Äf - fin kann

Refrain

LIED VON SCHLARAFFENLAND

Text by
GEORG KAISER

Music by
KURT WEILL

Molto animato (♩ = 104)

Es wächst uns in den
Was gut schmeckt,liegt auf

Mund der Wein, wir gra-ben in demWein-berg nicht und wis-sen nicht und wis-sen nicht,wer die
uns - remTisch, wo - her es kommtundwie mans holt, es wird ge-holt,es wird ge-holt und

Trau-ben von den Re-ben bricht. Wir sel - ber
noch was ek - kig ist,das rollt. Wir win - ken

rüh - ren kei - ne Hand wie im Schla-raf-fen-land,wie im Schla-raf-fen-land.
kaum mit ei - ner Hand wie im Schla-raf-fen-land,wie im Schla-raf-fen-land.

Lied von Schlaraffenland - 4 - 1

Lied von Schlaraffenland - 4 - 2

U. E. 10471

un - ten quetscht es breit_____ und ü - ber al - lem thront die al - te

Herr - lich - keit. So ü - ber - dau - ert al - len Wel - ten -

brand das e - wi-ge Schla-raf-fen land, das e - wi-ge Schla-raf-fen-land.

THE LITTLE GRAY HOUSE

Lyrics by
MAXWELL ANDERSON

Music by
KURT WEILL

The Little Gray House - 4 - 1

The Little Gray House - 4 - 2

The Little Gray House - 4 - 4

LONELY HOUSE

Lyrics by
LANGSTON HUGHES

Music by
KURT WEILL

L'istesso tempo (*with soft expression*)

Lone - ly house, lone - ly me!

Fun - ny, with so man - y neigh - bors, How lone - ly it can

be! Oh lone - ly street!

Lone - ly town! Fun - ny, you can be so

199

Lonely House - 5 - 4

LOST IN THE STARS

Lyrics by
MAXWELL ANDERSON

Music by
KURT WEILL

202

Lost in the Stars - 4 - 2

DER SILBERSEE

LOTTERIEAGENTS TANGO

Text by
GEORG KAISER

Music by
KURT WEILL

Lotterieagents Tango - 5 - 1

206

Lotterieagents Tango - 5 - 2

L.:Ag. *mf*
nug. Das kal - ku - liert die Kro - ne des Ge - winns:

L.:Ag.
Zins und Zin - ses-zins.

Lotterieagent
Trägst du ein Herz von Fleisch, er - här - te es zu Stein und

L.:Ag.
wund' - re dich nicht, wenn es nicht gleich ge - lingt. Sei ein - mal

208

L.:Ag. hart vor_ ei - ner gro-ßen Not, bald siehst du zu, wenn wer ins Was-ser

L.:Ag. springt; das ga -ran -tiert die Kro - ne des Ge - winns:

L.:Ag. Zins und Zin - ses-zins.

L.:Ag. Bau ei -nen Turm von_ Qua-dern um dich, du hörst nicht wie sie draußen kläglich

L.:Ag. schrein. Sei blind, sei taub, er-las-se kei - ne Schuld, du büßt ja Geld und Gel-des Nut -zen

Lotterieagents Tango - 5 - 4

L.-Ag.
ein, ver-leug-ne nie die Kro-ne des Ge-winns:
mf
f
Zins und Zin-ses-zins.
ff
Dar-um ler-ne, wie man's macht, daß ei-nem
Zin-ses-zins und Zin-ses-freu-de lacht.
ff
p
p
p

LOVE SONG

Lyrics by
ALAN JAY LERNER

Music by
KURT WEILL

Love Song - 6 - 1

Sing of how ev - er near the shore and sea, And that's how true love should ev - er be._____ I sing a song a - bout the snow fall,_____ Sing of how gen - tle is the snow - fall,_____

Love Song - 6 - 4

MACK THE KNIFE

Original German Lyrics by
BERTOLT BRECHT
English Lyrics by
MARC BLITZSTEIN

Music by
KURT WEILL

Mack the Knife - 2 - 1

Mack the Knife - 2 - 2

MARCH TO ZION

Text by
FRANZ WERFEL

Music by
KURT WEILL

March to Zion - 2 - 1

MARTERL

Lyrics by
BERTOLT BRECHT

Music by
KURT WEILL

Hier ruht_____ die
Die ro - te

Auch auf folgenden Text: Die

poco rit. *a tempo*

Marterl - 3 - 1

Jung - frau   Jo - han - na Beck.
Ro - sa   schon lang ver - schwand.

Als sie starb, war ih - re Un - schuld
Die ist tot,   ihr Auf - ent - halts - ort

schon vor - her weg.   Die Män -
ist un - be - kannt.   Weil

ner   ha - ben ihr den Rest_____ ge -
sie den Ar - men hat die Wahr - heit ge -

Marterl - 3 - 2

ge - - - ben, drum floh sie aus
sa - - - get, drum ha - ben sie die Rei - chen

die - sem sü - - - - - ßen Le - - ben.
aus dem Le - - - - ben ge - ja - - - get.

pp

Ru - he sanft,
Ru - he sanft,

pp

ru - he sanft._____
ru - he sanft._____

MATROSEN-TANGO

Lyrics by
BERTOLT BRECHT

Music by
KURT WEILL

Hal - loh,   jetzt fah - ren wir nach Bir - ma hin - ü - ber.   Whis-ky ha - ben wir ja noch ge -

nü - gend   da - bei.   Und Zi - gar - ren rau-chen wir   „Hen - ry Klay"

und die Mä - dels sind wir ja   auch schon ü - ber.   Na, da   sind wir e - ben jetzt__ so__

blik-ken, und dem lie - ben Gott, dem liegt vielleicht auch gar nichts da - ran, und wenn, dann muß er sich drein

schik-ken. Na al - so: Good-bye! Mit - „Mensch, bei mir nicht" und „Na wat denn, mein Sohn." Und

fehlt's wo, dann laß mich's mal wis - sen. Und 'ne fei - ne - re Re-gung nicht

um 'ne Mil - lion! Da wird eb'n auf al - les ge - pfif - fen! Und das Meer ist blau, so blau,

und das geht al - les sei - nen Gang. Und wenn die Cho - se aus ist,

dann fängt's von vor - ne an. Und das Meer ist blau, so blau

und das geht ja auch noch lang. Und das Meer ist blau, so blau,

und das Meer ist blau, so blau, und das Meer ist blau, so blau, das Meer ist blau.

The final scene of *The Eternal Road*, New York, 1937
The congregation is forced to leave the synagogue in search of a safe haven.

MAY AND JANUARY

Lyrics by
MAXWELL ANDERSON

Music by
KURT WEILL

MILE AFTER MILE

Lyrics by
BUDDY BERNIER
and CHARLES ALAN

Music by
KURT WEILL

Diagrams for Guitar Accomp.

Mile After Mile - 3 - 1

232

Mile After Mile - 3 - 3

JOHNNY JOHNSON

MON AMI, MY FRIEND

Lyrics by
PAUL GREEN

Music by
KURT WEILL

* *Names of chords for Ukulele and Banjo.*
Symbols for Guitar.

Mon Ami, My Friend - 4 - 1

MOON-FACED, STARRY-EYED

Lyrics by
LANGSTON HUGHES

Music by
KURT WEILL

Moon-Faced, Starry-Eyed - 3 - 1

MORITAT VOM MACKIE MESSER

Lyrics by
BERTOLT BRECHT

Music by
KURT WEILL

Blues-Tempo (♩=66)

(In der Art eines Leierkastens)

mf

Und der Hai-fisch, der hat Zäh - ne, und die trägt er im Ge-
schö - nen blau - en Sonn - tag liegt ein to - ter Mann am

sicht, und Mac-heath der hat ein Mes - ser, doch das Mes - ser
Strand und ein Mensch geht um die Ek - ke, den man Mak - kie

1.
2.

sieht man nicht. An 'nem
Mes - ser nennt. Und Schmul Mei - er bleibt ver-

p

schwun - den, und so man - cher rei - che Mann, und sein

LOVE LIFE

MR. RIGHT

Lyrics by
ALAN JAY LERNER

Music by
KURT WEILL

Mr. Right - 4 - 1

KONJUNKTUR

DIE MUSCHEL VON MARGATE

Lyrics by
FELIX GASBARRA

Music by
KURT WEILL

Allegro moderato

Gesang

1. In Mar-gate auf der Pro-me - nade hing ein
2. Mar-gate auf der Pro-me - nade er -
3. als der Tank zu pum-pen an-fing in Mar-
4. als die Son - ne am höch-sten stand in Mar-

Piano

1. ble - cher-nes La - den - schild vor ei - ner Bu - de mit Sou - ve - nirs ei - ne
2. hob sich ein Ge - stank. Wo einst die Bu - de mit Mu - scheln stand, steht
3. gate auf der Pro - me - nade, ein Dut - zend an je - dem Bohr-turm hing, der
4. gate auf der Pro - me - nade, da fing das Öl zu bren - nen an von

1. gro - ße Mu-schel im Bild. Da bot ein al - ter Mann be -
2. ein Pe - tro - le - um - Tank. Der Sohn von je - nem al - ten Mann fing
3. ü - ber Öl bei Ba - ku steht. Kolt - schak und De - ni - kin, da
4. A - ser - beidschan bis Ti - bet, es steck - te die Welt in Brand. Pe -

248

1. mal - te Mu - scheln an. Ganz Mar - gate kann - te sein Ge-bell:
2. ei - nen an-dern La - den an: ein Naph - ta= und Ben - zin - Kar-tell:
3. wur - de aus Blut Ben - zin; aus tau - send Häl - sen sprang der Quell:
4. tro - le - um heißt un-ser Va - ter - land, da - für zer-lö - chern wir uns das Fell:

1. Shell! Shell! Shell! Mu - schel von
2. Shell! Shell! Shell! Mu - schel von
3. Shell! Shell! Shell! Mu - schel von
4. Shell! Shell! Shell! Mu - schel von

1. Mar - gate bringt Ih - nen Glück, Mu - schel im gol - de - nen
2. Mar - gate brach-te ihm Glück, Mu - schel in gol - de - nem
3. Mar - gate bringt Ih - nen Glück, Mu - schel in gol - de - nem
4. Mar - gate bringt Ih - nen Glück, wir a - ber geh'n vor die

MY SHIP

Lyrics by
IRA GERSHWIN

Music by
KURT WEILL

Andantino cantabile

Piano — *mp*

Refrain

My ship has sails that are made of silk, The decks are trimmed with gold, And of jam and spice there's a par-a-dise in the hold. ___ My

* *Names of chords for Ukulele and Banjo.*
Symbols for Guitar.

My Ship - 3 - 1

ONE TOUCH OF VENUS (FILM)

MY WEEK

Lyrics by
ANN RONELL

Music by
KURT WEILL